NEW ORLEANS FURNITURE

THE KNAPP PRESS

PUBLISHERS

New Orleans Furniture
was created and produced by
REBUS, INC.
and published by THE KNAPP PRESS
5900 Wilshire Boulevard
Los Angeles, California 90036

ISBN 0-89535-154-4

In the late eighteenth and early nineteenth centuries, New Orleans furniture tended toward the simple—cypress, pine, or cherrywood pieces without ornamentation, but with subtle curves that echoed the French Provincial style. When booming commerce made New Orleans one of the country's wealthiest and most vibrant cities in the 1830s, newly rich citizens were ready for a style of furnishing that captured the spirit of their sudden success—the Rococo Revival.

"The utmost luxury of decoration" is the way one writer in 1850 described the furniture of the Rococo Revival, which was the height of fashion then in America and nowhere more than in New Orleans. The bold curves and exuberant ornaments of Rococo Revival furniture were inspired by French designs of the seventeenth and eighteenth centuries, and in the city that was still French in its soul, the furniture that recalled the glories of Louis XIV and Louis XV was avidly embraced. Furniture makers produced parlor and bedroom pieces with richly carved decorations—flowers, fruit, birds, cherubs, and shells. Vividly carved roses and clusters of grapes were especially popular. The carvings were enhanced by sumptuous upholstery of a rich masculine red or a demure feminine blue. Merchants popularized the idea of matching sets of furniture, an almost unheard-of extravagance formerly limited to the very rich. A large parlor might have two sofas facing a table, with as many as a dozen matching armchairs and side chairs arranged around the room. The permanent arrangement of furniture was another new idea—in the eighteenth century furniture had been pushed against the wall when not in use. Carefully arranged to facilitate conversation, these matching parlor sets with their numerous components made a striking impression—a profuse display of luxury. The high ceilings, lofty windows, and ample rooms of New Orleans houses made the perfect setting for these visually dramatic ensembles.

The premier maker of Rococo Revival furniture was probably John Henry Belter of New York, whose furniture was found in the most fashionable New Orleans parlors. Belter's work was a happy marriage of the machine and human craftsmanship. He patented a process for laminating and steaming rosewood to create distinctive sinuous shapes; but once the wood had been formed by machines, his artists went to work carving intricate, highly realistic floral decorations by hand. New Orleans buyers prized Belter's furniture not only for its elaborate beauty but for its sturdiness as well. His laminated rosewood remained firm after years of use and exposure to extreme humidity.

The two most prominent furniture makers in New Orleans itself were Prudent Mallard and François Seignouret. Seignouret was born in France in 1768 and first came to New Orleans as a wine dealer. In 1822 he opened a furniture shop in the French Quarter at 520 Royal Street. He specialized in the American Empire style of furniture, which was inspired by French Restauration furniture and characterized by large, plain surfaces without carved ornamentation, and a sense of massive scale.

Mallard was also born in France, in 1809. He emigrated to New York at the age of twenty and may have spent several years working there in the shop of Duncan Phyfe. He moved to New Orleans and set himself up in business as a furniture dealer in 1838 down the street from Seignouret at 67 Royal. His newspaper advertisements offered "Fancy Articles from Paris and London" and invited "Orders for Furniture, to be executed on special drawings...at moderate prices." He owned ships that carried cotton to Europe and came back with furniture and other luxury items.

His ships also sailed to the Caribbean and South America to acquire mahogany and rosewood for Mallard's own furniture.

In the 1840s and 1850s, New Orleans was booming and provided an eager market of wealthy and middle-class buyers for Seignouret, Mallard, Belter, John and Joseph W. Meeks of New York, and other furniture makers. Mallard and Seignouret produced furniture that can only be described as monumental—armoires ten feet high and beds eight or nine feet long and up to eight feet wide. Mallard is noted for his enormous beds, with silk-lined half canopies that were both decorative and practical—the canopy provided a place to hang mosquito netting. Mallard's bedroom sets often included a *duchesse*, a dressing table topped with marble. Marble was a popular material for dresser and table tops in New Orleans because it is cool to the touch.

In the mid-nineteenth century new revival styles became popular, including Gothic Revival and Renaissance Revival. The latter was based on sixteenth- and seventeenth-century French designs. New Orleans furniture makers, including Seignouret and Mallard, began to work in this style, which was elaborate but less sinuous than Rococo Revival. It featured incised carvings, medallions, and inlays.

The Renaissance and Gothic Revival styles did not completely supplant Rococo Revival in New Orleans. In the depressed years after the Civil War, New Orleanians could not afford to invest in new furniture. The homes that had been furnished before the war remained frozen in time. Rococo Revival furniture, prized before the war as the "union of lightness, elegance, and grace," became an even more treasured reminder of a happier past.

A PORTFOLIO OF NEW ORLEANS FURNITURE

A Louisiana cabinetmaker probably fashioned this armoire in the eighteenth or early nineteenth century. This commodious armoire, almost seven feet high and five feet wide, displays cabriole legs with scrolled feet and curved panels typical of the Louis XV style. Made of mahogany and Spanish cedar, the piece is now in the Louisiana State Museum.

The unadorned but graceful lines of this small table, in Pitot House, are typical of New Orleans furniture of the eighteenth and early nineteenth century. The table was fashioned of mahogany and has scalloped skirts.

The New Orleans furniture maker François Seignouret is noted for designing a distinctive type of chair in the Empire style. Called Seignouret chairs, they are remarkably graceful—with their scrolled arms and modified cabriole legs—and exceptionally comfortable. Seignouret sold these chairs with two interchangeable seats, a velvet cushion for the winter, and a cane seat for the warm months. This example is in Hermann-Grima House.

This laminated rosewood ladies' chair, in Gallier House, has been attributed to John Henry Belter. The covering is pale blue silk damask. Ladies' chairs were made without arms so that women in hoopskirts could sit comfortably in them.

4

The méridienne is a couch designed for reclining. It was ideal for a midday nap, or simply for a lady to relax in when she was wearing a hoopskirt. When the bustle became fashionable later in the nineteenth century, this form of furniture went out of style— a woman wearing a bustle could not settle comfortably into a méridienne. This méridienne is in Gallier House.

John Henry Belter may have been the maker of this laminated rosewood chair, with delicate cut-out ornamentation of C and S curves. This chair, in Gallier House, is upholstered in blue velvet.

Delicately painted floral motifs adorn the sides of a game table in Gallier House, seen here in detail. The style of the decorations, which include gold leaf and inlaid mother-of-pearl, suggest that the table was made in England about 1855. The top opens to reveal a chess board, and there are compartments in the sides to hold pieces.

The Gilbert Company of Boston made this rosewood baby grand piano, now in 1850 House, about 1855. It is a rare type, specially designed for small apartments, known as a cocked-hat piano because the strings are arranged at a forty-five-degree angle.

This handsome laminated rosewood armchair in 1850 House has been attributed to John Henry Belter of New York. It was probably made in the early 1850s.

9

The C and S curves on the back of the Belter chair, here in detail, frequently appear on furniture of the Rococo Revival. At the center of the crest is a small, realistically carved rose blossom.

The New York furniture makers John and Joseph W. Meeks may have fashioned this laminated rosewood table in 1850 House. The ornate openwork decoration is typical of the Rococo Revival.

Prudent Mallard fashioned this duchesse—*a marble-topped dressing table—as part of a rosewood bedroom set for Isabel Puig of 624 Royal Street. A pair of cases for cosmetics, also topped with marble, flank the mirror. The set is now in 1850 House.*

This magnificent bed is part of the Puig bedroom set made by Mallard. The carvings, flutes, moldings, and outlines of this rosewood bed are highlighted in lemonwood—an imaginative and highly unusual decorative technique.

13

This detail of the Mallard bed in 1850 House reveals the beautiful coloristic effect Mallard achieved by combining rosewood and lemonwood.

A delicate swan's neck supports the mosquito netting over this rosewood crib in 1850 House. The crib was made in Louisiana between 1845 and 1860 by a local craftsman.

15

CREDITS

Photography by Karen Radkai

The Editors would like to thank the following for their assistance:
Timothy J. Chester, chief curator, Lousiana State Museum; Ann M.
Masson, director, Gallier House.

Picture Editor: Mary Z. Jenkins; Editor: Vance Muse; Designer: Ronald
Gross; Writer: Henry Wiencek; Production: Paul Levin; Managing Editor:
Fredrica Harvey